Hope in a Time of Despair

Hope in a Time of Despair

A CAREGIVER'S
JOURNEY OF FAITH

PATRICIA SEWARD GRAHAM

CITI OF
BOOKS

CITIOFBOOKS, INC.
3736 Eubank NE Suite A1
Albuquerque, NM 87111-3579
www.citiofbooks.com
Hotline: 1 (877) 389-2759
Fax: 1 (505) 930-7244

Ordering Information:
Quantity sales. Special discounts are available on quantity purchases by corporations, associations, and others. For details, contact the publisher at the address above.

Printed in the United States of America.

ISBN-13:   Softcover   979-8-89391-057-5
            eBook   979-8-89391-058-2

Library of Congress Control Number: 2024907639

Table of Contents

June 17, 2021

HOPE IN A TIME OF DESPAIR- A CAREGIVER'S JOURNEY OF FAITH

1. INTRODUCTION

Have you ever been in a situation where you thought there was no way out? Have you ever felt that your problems were closing in on you? Have you exhausted all of your resources and you don't know where to turn? Have you ever felt as if no one listened to you or understood what you were going through? Has the advice you've received left you with more questions than answers?

Caregiving can be stressful when you have responsibility for providing for the needs of another person. Often times you are placed in a caregiving role, not by choice, but by circumstance. You often have to sacrifice your wants or needs for the sake of another, but when you care for someone, the rewards of ensuring someone's wellbeing outweigh the sacrifices that are made. One must remember to keep faith and trust in God that things will work out, no matter how difficult the tasks involved.

This book is dedicated to anyone who is in a caregiving role, or anyone who believes that they are in a difficult situation and there appears no solution to their problem. I hope you will be inspired to keep the faith and never lose hope. Without hope, life has no meaning. Remember there is always light at the end of the tunnel!

Scriptures for Difficult Moments

Scriptures can help you get through a difficult moment. Try repeating one or some of your favorites to get through the trying moment. Here are some that may help you reflect on God's unwavering concern for what you are going through.

"God is our refuge and strength, a very present help in trouble." Psalms 46:1 KJV

"May the God of hope fill you with all joy and peace as you trust in him, so that you may overflow with hope by the power of the Holy Spirit." Romans 15:13 NIV

"Trust in the Lord with all thine heart; and lean not unto thine own understanding. In all thy ways acknowledge him, and he shall direct thy paths." Proverbs 3:5-6 KJV

"Be joyful in hope, patient in affliction, faithful in prayer." Romans 12:12 NIV

"But those who hope in the Lord will renew their strength. They will soar on wings like eagles; they will run and not grow weary; they will walk and not be faint." Isaiah 40:31 NIV

"Do not be anxious about anything, but in every situation, by prayer and petition, with thanksgiving, present your requests to God." Philippians 4:6 NIV

Commit yourself to the Lord; trust in him, and he will act. Psalm 37:5 (NRSV)

What then are we to say about these things? If God is for us, who is against us? Romans 8:31 (NRSV)

Let us hold fast to the confession of our hope without wavering, for he who has promised is faithful. Hebrews 10:23 (NRSV)

A Time of Celebration

October 2003 was going to be the beginning of a new chapter in our lives. We were looking forward to becoming empty nesters and rediscovering ourselves as a couple. We had dropped our daughter off at college (woo- hoo!) and looked forward to celebrating our 30th wedding anniversary. Atlantic City, New Jersey was our favorite place to visit so we planned to celebrate there. My friend Jane (RIP) allowed us to use her timeshare for this occasion. We decided to make it a relaxing time with a stopover in Virginia.

We couldn't ask for better weather at the beginning of our trip. No rain, pleasant temperature in the 70's. Plenty of sunshine. Moderate traffic although speeders are always on the highway. The timeshare was located near the boardwalk, within walking distance of the casinos. It was very comfortable, spacious and relaxing. The jacuzzi was so enticing.

One of the features that kept us going back to Atlantic City was the freebies. In previous years, we had won so many good freebies, especially when listening to promotions about real estate ventures. Of course, during this stay, we signed up for one of the tours and the 90-minute presentation.

The Stroke

The presentation was about purchasing a timeshare. We had no plans to buy one, but we listened to the presenter anyway. I don't remember what the prize was for listening, so after much persuasion from the presenter, we decided it was time to leave. My husband started complaining about having a headache and when I looked over at him, he was sweating profusely. When I asked him if he was okay; he said he was, just tired from the long ride. We decided to go back to the room to rest for the evening comedy show. The comedian was very good, and we had an enjoyable time. My husband was feeling better and there were no other signs that things were going awry. I prepared our dinner and after eating, decided to relax in the Jacuzzi. It was refreshing to wind down after a long ride and listening to a presentation. My husband didn't want to get in the jacuzzi, but I enticed him to give it a try and relax. After much coaching, he decided to try.

After a few minutes, I noticed that he appeared to be getting weak. I asked if he was okay, and he was able to respond yes. All of a sudden, he started to slip down in the jacuzzi, his arm became weak, and his speech became slurred. I tried to help him up, to no avail. I became frantic and called the front desk to ask for assistance. I was so thankful that someone would come up to assist in getting him out and into the bed.

Stroke was not something that I had entertained was happening. After trying to determine what was going on with my husband and his inability to tell me how he was feeling, I said to my husband, "Honey, I think you're having a stroke". My husband is typical of many males who will do almost anything to avoid going to a doctor. I suggested that he needed to go to the hospital, but he didn't want to. However, I called 911 and after a few minutes, paramedics arrived. They evaluated my husband and suggested that he be taken to the hospital for treatment. I was in a state of panic and disbelief, not wanting to believe this was happening. As they were preparing to lift him on the stretcher for transport, I began to pray, "Lord, please let him be okay".

I arrived at the hospital's emergency room soon after the paramedics had dropped him off. I inquired as to his whereabouts and if there was an update on his condition. No information was readily available, and he was still being evaluated. Emergency rooms are places of long waits and can be nerve wracking when information is slow to come. It seems as if I was waiting forever before any information was available. After several intense hours of waiting, I was told that my husband would be admitted to the hospital due to suffering a stroke. Feelings of disbelief, anxiety, worry set in. How could this happen? Did I miss the warning signs? Where do I go from here how? Is he going to be okay? How do we move forward from here? What's going to be different going forward?

As I reflect on what transpired prior to the Medics arriving, I ask myself what should have given me indications that something was wrong? In reviewing the five warning signs of stroke, were any of the symptoms present:

1. sudden onset of weakness or numbness on one side of the body,

2. sudden speech difficulty or confusion

3. difficulty seeing in one or both eyes,

4. sudden onset of dizziness or trouble walking or loss of balance

5. sudden severe headache with no known cause.

1) https://www.cdc.gov > stroke > signs…

Yes, the signs were there, but if you're not looking for anything to go wrong, your thoughts are not in that direction. It's easy to be told to look for warning signs, but you have to be aware that someone is in a compromising situation. Although the situation looked grim, I was prayerful that God was there with me and would be my support system.

After waiting anxiously in the waiting room for several hours, the doctor called me into the office. He showed me the scan of my husband's brain. According to the scan, my husband had a brain aneurysm on the left side below the middle of the brain. The doctor was concerned about the bleed that was present, and his outlook on the situation was not a positive one. He asked if I knew what my husband's wishes were if he became incapacitated. The doctor explained that my husband would be put on life support, and if at any point he stopped breathing, what measures would he want to be put in place to revive him. Would he want to be resuscitated, knowing that any use of CPR and a defibrillator may result in ribs being injured? As you can imagine, such discussion was difficult to listen to and seemed to imply that all hope was gone. But I reminded myself that I serve a God who is able to do the unexpected.

"Now unto him that is able to do exceeding abundantly above all that we ask or think, according to the power that worketh in us" (Ephesians 3:20 KJV)

As I sat there pondering what to do, I remembered that my husband and I had recently been talking about what measures we wanted to put in place if we were faced with an unforeseen medical emergency. His wishes were to have everything that could possibly be done to save his life be implemented. We also talked about his father being kept on life support for nine months because his mother was unable to make the decision to remove life support. Although I was and still am unsure of my wishes, I respected his decision, not knowing that I would be faced with a situation where I would have to make that decision. I informed the doctor that my husband and I had recently had such a conversation and that his wish was to do whatever possible to save his life.

Over the course of the next two days, little had changed in my husband's condition. My stay at the time share in Atlantic City was up and I had to return back home to Charlotte. As I looked at my husband in that hospital room – unresponsive, eyes rolling around unfocused, tubes seemingly everywhere – my heart was truly broken. Although I was speaking to him about my love, praying for improvement, I wasn't sure if he knew who I was, if he knew his wife was there, if I would be back to see him again. As I drove down the highway, I received a call from the hospital. You could imagine what the first response would be, this is not good. I was near a convenience store and was able to pull over to converse with the nurse. My husband was having problems breathing and permission was being requested to do a tracheotomy and most likely surgery was needed to institute tube feeding. Permission was granted.

As I continued on my drive back home, I talked to God most of the way. My first conversation was a prayer for a safe journey on the 8-9 hour trip alone and for recovery for my husband. Most of my conversation with God was to remind Him of His promises. I spoke to God as if I was speaking to a friend. I reminded him that He promised never to leave me alone; that He said if we needed anything, all we had to do was ask in His name, and He would deliver. I reminded God that He was a healer. He healed the sick, the lame, the blind; He raised Lazarus and others from the dead. Surely, He could heal my husband. I reminded God that He created my husband, that He knew all about him and asked God if He would spare my husband's life. I felt better after my conversation with God and was hopeful that things would work out in my husband's favor.

"When thou passest through the waters, I will be with thee; and through the river, they shall not overflow thee; when thou walkest through the fire, thou shalt not be burned; neither shall the flame kindle upon thee." Isaiah 43:2 KJV

I would encourage you to talk with God when confronted with a difficult situation. Find a quiet place that gives you comfort, where there are no distractions. Pretend that you are talking with your best friend about what is happening. You just want your friend to listen while you speak, not to make judgment, but just listen. If you want advice, ask God to provide you with His will and to guide you with an open mind to receive any revelation he places within your spirit. You also have to be willing to listen and accept the direction in which things are moving, although you may not agree or understand why.

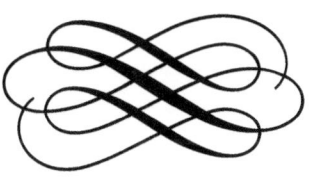

Calls to Family

While in Atlantic City, I called family members to let them know about my husband's stroke and his condition was not good. I asked for prayer for his recovery. My sister who lived in Maryland went to visit him and although she wanted to be hopeful, I could sense in her voice that she was not expecting a favorable outcome. His sister also visited but came to the same conclusion. I remained hopeful and prayerful for his recovery and continued my conversations with God.

Your family will support you when going through difficult times, but they may not always understand the strain you are going through. You may not always want to burden your family with your problems because after all, they have their problems too. Don't add pressure on yourself when you are not able to get what you need from family or friends. They can only provide you with the limited resources that they have. Be grateful for what ever assistance is offered and continue to do the best that you can.

Hospital Stay

During the days my husband remained in the hospital, the nursing staff was comforting. They would put the phone to his ear and allow me to talk with him. He was not able to speak but they assured me that he was hearing my voice. I would tell him "Don't give up honey; fight as hard as you can; you can make it; everything will be okay; just don't give up!" As time progressed, the nurse would say that his eyes seemed to light up when he heard my voice. Those were words that kept me going and encouraged me to remain hopeful. I asked my co-workers to pray for my husband. If there was anyone that I had an opportunity to speak with, I would ask them if they believed in prayer, and would ask them to pray for my husband. I am a firm believer in prayer, and I strongly believe that prayer changes things. There were so many prayers being made on behalf of my husband, that I knew a healing was going to happen.

I was able to visit my husband around Thanksgiving due to two church members blessing me with money for a bus trip to Atlantic City. God is so God. He knows what you need before you ask Him. Fortunately, the bus terminal was within walking distance from the hospital. When I arrived to see my husband, I wasn't sure what to expect. When I entered the hospital room, my husband was surprised to see me, and I was surprised to see him as well. He appeared thinner than I remembered, he was unable to communicate (diagnosis of aphasia – loss of ability to understand or express speech, caused by brain damage); he had a breathing tube, was being given IVs, and was being tube fed. We couldn't embrace, but we were able to hold hands and I could rub his face. I gave thanks to God because my husband was still alive and more aware than when I last saw him. I visited with him that Thanksgiving weekend, leaving me more encouraged about his condition.

"Heal me, O Lord, and I shall be healed; save me, and I shall be saved: for thou art my praise" Jeremiah 17:14 KJV

While I was there, I spoke with the social worker who asked me if there were any plans for my husband's care once he is released from the hospital. She suggested that I start looking for a nursing home. Although I am a social worker myself and accustomed to helping others, when you're confronted with the same scenario, your situation takes on a different meaning. You are no longer the helper, but you have become the person needing help. Not only was there a need to locate a nursing home, there were other things to consider;

- Insurance won't pay for nursing home care.

- We don't have long term care insurance; how would the cost of long-term care be paid for?

- How was my husband going to be transported from New Jersey to North Carolina; what would be the cost of transport?

- Would there be space available in a nursing home to accept him?

I was becoming overwhelmed. In addition to working full time, I had the unexpected task of finding appropriate care for my husband upon his discharge from the hospital. I had become a caregiver, a family caregiver who is described as someone who takes care of a family member without pay.

When I returned back home to Charlotte, my initial task was to start exploring nursing facilities to determine the services offered to residents in their care. My priority was to find a facility that was close to home so I wouldn't have far to travel. I wanted a place close to my job in case of emergency and if I needed to get there quickly. Although there is sometimes controversy over nursing home care, nursing homes provide a needed service for someone in need of 24-hour supervision and care. It would be ideal to care for someone at home, but if you are not able or capable of providing care for a loved one, release your feelings of guilt and recognize your inability to care for that person. If your loved one progresses to a point where you are able to care for them, you can then bring them home to provide that care.

Once I selected the nursing homes to consider, I referred the information to the hospital social worker to have available when my husband was ready for discharge. I continued to speak with my husband during his stay at the hospital, encouraging him to be strong, telling of my love for him, and a desire to return home. His condition, although improved, was still in an unstable situation. Breathing was difficult and he required a breathing tube, the trachea was still in place, he was on a feeding tube, he was unable to speak or communicate effectively, and he was too weak to walk.

I was told that my husband could not travel by bus due to his condition and would need to be transported by air. In my search for air travel, the cost to fly him to Charlotte would cost $6000.

I tried to get assistance from family and church to no avail. I became hopeful when I learned that there was a charitable group that could provide transport for free, but my hope was dashed because it was determined that he would need medical assistance during the trip because of his condition. Fortunately, I was able to take a loan from my retirement account, although there would not be much left, in order to pay for air transport. I was thankful that I did have this resource to rely upon in getting him home.

I will never forget that phone call on Christmas Eve of 2003 informing me that my husband had arrived safely at the nursing home. Praises be to God that He made a way for my husband's recovery to begin. I would visit with my husband daily after leaving work, and on weekends. There were several crises along the way. Problems developed with the feeding tube which required surgery. During surgery, the surgeon discovered that the feeding tube had not been placed correctly and the correction was made. If not, there could have been serious complications in the future which would have resulted in the feeding tube being permanent. Our goal was to eventually have the feeding tube removed. Thank you, Lord, for your intervention!

Another crisis was dealing with infections which resulted in having to see an infection specialist for treatment. Infections can sometimes be a frequent problem for residents in nursing homes. There were frequent visits for treatment, but eventually the infection was cleared up. My faith in God's healing power remained strong and I kept believing that no matter the situation, I would remain faithful to my trust in God.

"Therefore I say unto you, What things soever you desire, when ye pray, believe that ye receive them, and ye shall have them." Mark 11:24 KJV

"And call upon me in the day of trouble: I will deliver thee, and thou shalt glorify me." Psalm 50:15 KJV

Still another crisis resulted in a referral to a throat doctor who thought there was throat cancer. In my prayers to God, I denounced the doctor's diagnosis and would not entertain cancer as a possibility. I am not a doctor, but I did not detect any symptoms that would lead to there being cancer. As Christians, we have been endowed with the Holy Spirit who is there to guide us in our quest for answers to difficult problems. The Holy Spirit is there to advise and help us discern information that has been presented so that we can make informed decisions. I believe that the Holy Spirit was guiding me in seeking a second opinion. In so doing, cancer was ruled out. Thank you, Jesus, for the gift of the Holy Spirit!

"And I will ask the father, and he will give you another advocate to help you and be with you forever-the Spirit of truth. John 14:16-17 (NIV)

When we were dealing with throat concerns, I inquired about the possibility of the trachea being removed. The doctor agreed that it could be removed, so our next step was to include this in the plan of care. Once the trachea was removed and the feeding tube was removed, my husband had to undergo a test to determine his ability to swallow. Therapy was implemented to build strength to swallow so that he could be introduced to solid foods in his diet. Slowly, my husband was able to eat solid foods again and he could begin to build strength and stamina to receive physical therapy.

During the course of the next several months, physical therapy continued with progress being made to maneuver him in the wheelchair. My husband was still aphasic, but understood what was said, although he could not speak or converse normally. He was able to transfer from wheelchair to chair with assistance. Although he was totally paralyzed on his right side, mobility on his left side allowed him to have limited movement.

He would need assistance with activities of daily living, such as bathing, dressing, meal preparation, and other functions. I failed to mention that while nursing home visits were being made daily, I was still working a full-time job. I also accompanied him to medical appointments so that I could keep up with his medical condition and be alert to any problems that might occur. As I stated earlier, caregiving can be stressful and requires dedication and commitment. It is important to take care of yourself and recognize your limitations. You need to seek out resources in the community that will enable you to carry out your responsibilities to the best of your ability. I recognized that I would need help if I was going to be able to bring him home, so I sought out resources to assist with his needs. My husband remained in the nursing home for over a year.

During my employment, I participated on an advisory committee of a program that provides services to adults who needed nursing home placement, but the family wanted to care for the person at home. This program is called the Community Alternatives Program (referred to as CAP). I made an application, and my husband was accepted into the program. I was able to coordinate his discharge from the nursing home with the date CAP services could begin so that I would have coverage once he returned home. Part of his plan of care was for him to attend Adult Day Care so that I could continue to work, and he would receive supervision during the day.

I brought my husband home on a weekend, and I had to provide for his care. I expected there to be challenges and of course there were. I had to provide for his personal care, bathing, dressing, assisting with transfers. Nighttime was tedious because I had to transfer him from the sofa where he spent the day to the bed. I made the adjustments and eventually became adept at providing his care. When you love someone with whom you have spent 30 years of marriage, sacrifices are made if that relationship has been one of mutual respect and caring. After all, the marriage vows include "in sickness and in health".

Once CAP services were started, things went well, although the aides changed frequently. There is always an adjustment period because you have to get used to personalities and how people like to perform their tasks, but we survived. My husband was able to attend adult day care while I worked.

Things were going well for several years when the unexpected happened in April 2013. One night, while checking on my husband, I found hm to be somewhat unresponsive, and his eyes were fixated. I immediately called 911, Medic arrived, and he was transported to the hospital. After I got dressed, I went to the hospital, not knowing what may have transpired since he left home, praying all the way. Of course, doom and despair enveloped me, but I was praying that whatever happened, my husband would overcome this setback.

When the doctor completed his assessment, it was determined that my husband had suffered a seizure and another stroke. His condition was not as grave as the first stroke, but he remained in the hospital for approximately a week and was then transferred to a nursing home. This stroke weakened his left side, which impacted his ability to assist with his transfers. He again experienced difficulty with swallowing and had to have a tube inserted for feeding.

While at the nursing home he received the usual care, including physical therapy, occupational therapy, and training to determine if he would be able to swallow. At one point, the therapist indicated that he would always need the feeding tube, but that was not something I was willing to entertain. This is where prayer, faith, and trust in God come into play.

When talking to God, you have to make your requests known. Remind him of His promises to be with you through every situation, recognizing that all things are according to His will, but believing and trusting in Him to deliver. Remind yourself that God is faithful with new mercies every day. My prayer was for my husband to regain his ability to eat solid foods again. I was present during the swallowing therapy, encouraging along the way. I was so relieved when he was evaluated during the swallowing assessment, and it was determined that the feeding tube could be removed! Hallelujah! Praises to God for his mercy and blessings.

My husband remained in the nursing home for almost six to seven months before returning home. I had retired by this time and was able to provide care until CAP services could begin again. It took almost a month to get services back, but I managed his care and was so grateful when services started. During this time of caring for my husband, my father became ill. He had been living independently but was diagnosed with dementia. One evening, I received a call to go and check on him at his apartment. When I arrived, the apartment floor was flooded. Apparently, my dad had left the water running in his kitchen sink, and there was water everywhere. He said that he was waiting for his grandson to come and take him somewhere, which turned out not to be true. Since he could not remain in the apartment under those conditions, I decided to bring him home with me until nursing home placement could be secured. I didn't know how I was going to manage caring for two disabled people, but prayerfully, I was able to pull through. Relying on strength from God, trusting in his faithfulness to provide for my needs, a nursing home placement was found in about two weeks. I wish that I could have kept him at home with me, but I recognized my limitations, and Dad understood my dilemma of caring for my husband. I visited Dad regularly to ensure his needs were being met. Dad had been on dialysis for several years, and his primary concern was to receive his dialysis treatments. The day before he died, he kept repeating, "I've got to get to dialysis." As Dad was nearing the end of his life, I was with him on the night of his death. I read scriptures to him, not sure if he heard me or knew I was there. I wanted to stay with him as he drew his last breath, but his shallow breathing continued for a long time. I think that he did not want me to witness his passing, and shortly after I arrived back home, I received the call that he had passed away.

Dad was a firm believer in God and the scriptures that I read to him were my favorites: "Nay, in all these things we are more than conquerors through him that loved us. For I am persuaded , that neither death, nor life, nor angels, nor principalities, nor powers, nor things present, nor things to come, nor height, nor depth, nor any other creature, shall be able to separate us from the love of God, which is in Christ Jesus our Lord." (Romans 8:37–39 (KJV).

We were in a place of stability and hopeful that no crisis would come upon us in the near future. We celebrated forty-eight years of marriage and made the most of each day God granted us together. I try not to think about what could have been when I hear of persons who have suffered strokes and died from them. Through God's grace and mercy, he allowed us to survive the storms that came our way. I am forever grateful for the care received, medical professionals, and most importantly, to the aides who provided the hands-on care. One of my favorite songs testifies to God's faithfulness as I praise him for bringing us through the challenges we endured. To God be the glory!!!

Great Is Thy Faithfulness

Great is thy faithfulness, O God my Father, there is no turning of shadow with thee.

Thou changest not, thy compassions they fail not, as thou has been thou forever wilt be.

Great is thy faithfulness, great is thy faithfulness, Morning by morning new mercies I see.

All I have needed thy hand hath provided, Great is thy faithfulness, Lord unto me.

(Thomas Obadiah Chisholm, lyricist)

"This I recall to my mind, therefore I have hope. It is of the Lord's mercies that we are not consumed, because his compassions fail not. They are new every morning: Great is thy faithfulness." (Lamentations 3:21–23)

About the Author

Mrs. Graham was married to the love of her life, Meredith Graham, Jr., who is the inspiration for this book. They were married for forty-eight years and have one daughter, Michelle Graham. Mrs. Graham is a graduate of North Carolina Central University in Durham, North Carolina, with a bachelor's degree in Sociology. She has a Master of Social Work degree from the University of North Carolina in Chapel Hill, North Carolina. Mrs. Graham has been involved in many community activities during her career. She has served on the Board of Directors for the Southern Piedmont Chapter of the Alzheimer's Association and participated in the speaker's bureau for Alzheimer's disease. She also chaired a Minority Task Force on Alzheimer's disease to enhance awareness of the disease in minority communities and conducted workshops for families impacted by the disease. She also facilitated caregiver support groups for individuals in caregiving roles. Mrs. Graham retired from the Mecklenburg County Department of Social Services after thirty-three years of service. After retirement, she co-founded and served as Executive Director of the Raising Academic Performance (RAP) after school program to improve the graduation rate of at- risk youth. Mrs. Graham has served in various ministries of the church, including Family Life Ministry, editor of the church newsletter, and usher board, having once been recognized as District Usher of the year.

She is currently Superintendent of the Sunday Church School Department. One of her favorite scriptures for meditation are Romans 8:38–39, "For I am persuaded, that neither death, nor life, nor angels, nor principalities, nor powers, nor things present, nor things to come, nor height, nor depth, nor any other creature, shall be able to separate us from the love of God, which is in Christ Jesus our Lord."

In Loving Memory

On March 5, 2022, Meredith Graham, Jr., my husband, and soul mate of forty-eight years passed away. Without hope, we would not have been blessed to spend an additional eighteen years together after his strokes. Now our hope is assured in knowing that we will see each other again in that glorious place called heaven.

Rest in peace, my love. Until we meet again.

Pat

www.ingramcontent.com/pod-product-compliance
Lightning Source LLC
Chambersburg PA
CBHW051651120626
46551CB00015B/2319